To Dear Janet & Lloyd

Lovingly,

Mum & Dad

"In all thy ways acknowledge Him, and He shall direct thy paths." Prov. 3:6

I Love You

By Marlee & Ben Alex
Photos by Ben Alex

BETHANY HOUSE PUBLISHERS
MINNEAPOLIS, MINNESOTA 55438

Published for the U.S. and Canada by
Bethany House Publishers
Minneapolis, Minnesota

Acknowledgements
All pictures supplied by Ben Alex, Copenhagen

All Bible quotations from the New International Version,
copyright © 1978 by New York International Bible Society

Printed in Italy by New Interlitho S.P.A.,Milan

ISBN 0-87123-262-6

Contents:

The Magic of Love

I love you — a feeling that has been repeated down through history. Repeated even through my own life. But this is different. The center of my life is moved outside myself. I love you. Those words seem so insignificant compared to the ecstasy I feel. I feel passionate attraction. I want you to be mine. And I want to sacrifice myself for you.

A breeze in the trees. The wind in your hair. You fill up the emptiness in my lonely heart. I need what you have. I feel the security in belonging. You feel the same, and that gives us a strong feeling of oneness. Each of us possesses what the other promises in the way of delights, security and shared feelings. I am startled over the enormity of the gift I possess and the challenge it involves.

Sometimes I shrink from the insecurity of not being acceptable in your eyes. Sometimes the eye is a telescope. Sometimes it is a microscope. I am afraid you will find something you do not like. In a way, falling in love is playing hide-and-seek till we find total security. I feel tempted to hide my real self and pretend something that isn't really me.

Please, help me dare to be myself. Enter the backyard of my soul and tell me what you see on the other side.

Bo

4

$\mathcal{W}$e met hopefully on a spring day. My girlfriend had met you before and told me about you. You had seen my photo somewhere. It wasn't love at first sight. But you charmed me. By the end of a week we were in love. We sat barefoot in the grass and you gently tickled the bottom of my foot. I told you about my childhood fantasies. You made me laugh, and made my heart tingle with excitement. "Me" was becoming "us."

Your eyes were blue. Not deep blue, but deep. I felt depths in your soul even though you didn't let me see very much those days. I believed in you. I admired you. I felt ecstatic in the discovery of your attraction to me. We shared with each other things about our past. I wanted to be part of your future. The longing grew.

Sometimes I felt inferior and unsure. But I accepted the present with joy, anyway. I didn't want to miss out on a moment of this magic. Sometimes I felt disappointed in something you said or even the way you combed your hair. But the magic of the feeling and the knowing of what was happening to us, and most of all the power of my belief in you overcame that. You were not only a possibility in yourself. I saw in you my possibility — my unique, never-to-come-again possibility. We couldn't let each other go.

"Do not arouse
or awaken love
until it so desires."
Song of Songs 8:4

High Standards

I am aware that feelings are not eternal. They may come and go. Only truth can stand the test of times.

Let us lay the foundation of truth in our relationship. The standards we have now shall become the standards we have later on. The seed we sow now shall become what we harvest later on.

I love you, and I want to act on that love by mastering my selfish desires. What I believe is more important than what I feel.

The day we met I was attracted to your physical appearance. But I began to see the real you. I want to protect you and make you a whole person. We can only win together.

The days we were apart it occurred to me what a risk we are taking. Something in me wanted to stay single, waiting for a better opportunity. But the peace about "us" overwhelmed me. I knew we were right for each other, and I want to act on that assurance.

When I talked to your dad about us, he said, "Well, take good care of her, Ben, she's a sensitive girl. Whatever happens, keep a pure heart!"

Love in the long direction comes from purity rather than feelings.

Ben

We're engaged. I'm on cloud nine now. The memory of another day in your love sings me to sleep every night. I wake up thinking about your eyes.

How did it all begin? That night I will never forget. We didn't know each other well, but the admiration was growing. Our friendship was delicate. I saw you walking off in the distance. And someone whispered in my heart, "Would you be willing to give up your own ambitions to be Ben's wife? Would you be willing to rearrange your own priorities and desires?" With a moment's hesitation I said, "Yes, Lord." Still, I wondered if it wasn't the Lord's question at all, but my own.

And even if it was the Lord, I questioned Him, "But, Lord, why do you bother asking? Ben has no interest in me." And I determined to forget about it, about the possibility of "us".

That very evening you came to me and asked if we could talk. My knees started knocking. And as it turned out, you were interested. The Lord's quiet voice had prepared my heart for your question. I was thankful for that. And I was thankful He was a part of the whole thing before it began. And I'm thankful that our in-love-ness grew out of His wisdom.

And "the wisdom from above is first pure..." May His purity be our guiding light throughout our engagement days.

9

"How can
a young man
keep his way pure?
By living
according to your word."

Psalms 119:9

We are different. But we must not let the difference come between us. To you our wedding is a beginning. To me it's an ending. I think; you talk. I like ideas; you like people.

We must share our shortcomings, longings and dreams. I want to know what you expect of life. What do you expect from me?

Somebody asked me, "Why are you sure she and you are right for each other?" I said that I loved you. He said, "Later on you will need a better answer. The days will come when everything else seems to say: It was a mistake!"

He made me think. How can we nurture love?

I want to explore some questions with you. Are we compatible? What goals do we have? What moral standards? What spiritual visions and callings? Are we compatible intellectually and emotionally?

Our compatibilities give us security. Our incompatibilities are the differences that help us grow.

Be

Marriage

These busy days, planning the details of our wedding — the clothes, the music, our vows; it seems to me that some people never think much further than that.

But let's you and I enjoy planning together the details of our marriage as well.

The desire of my heart is that this sense of romance, this willingness to please, and this harmony we feel together might last our whole lives long. I want to build something eternal together with you. Please, share your wildest dreams with me. Tell me what you love to eat, what left hurts in you when you were a child. Tell me who you admire and what you enjoy more than anything else in the world. Tell me what makes you tell secrets.

I know that communication and compatibility are much more than these things, but it's a beginning. I want to begin to see what is likeable in the things you like. I want to see into the core of you which you keep hidden from most other people.

And even when I disagree with you, when I've tried to participate in your world and still feel estranged, I will pray for the grace to stand aside and let you be you. I trust your love, and that of the Lord so much that I will be willing to allow our differences to be.

"Two are better than one,
because they have a good
return for their work:
If one falls down,
his friend can help him up."

Ecclesiastes 4:9-10

Becoming One

"For this cause a man shall leave his father and mother and shall cleave to his wife..."

Today we have become one flesh! When I promised to love you and to cherish you, a strange thing happened. The last hidden fears shattered. For the first time I made a serious promise and gave myself totally. Now I belong to you.

And still, I carry the wounds, the mistakes of the past, with me. I'm sorry I have to give those to you, too. But they are part of me.

I no longer belong to my family or myself. I'm free in a new way. And at the same time, I'm bound in a new way — symbolized by the ring I wear.

Even though I love my family, I'm no longer dependent on them. I will never have to run back to them. And I will never have to run away from them. I belong to you.

Be

And the two shall become one flesh."

You are gentle and patient with me. But nothing is so strong as your gentleness. Personality and spirituality I've understood as a single girl, but sexuality is a new dimension. I have a feeling it will take many more days than our honeymoon to explore and feel comfortable with it, as well as to integrate it into our power to love, and our patterns of loving.

I want to fly on your wave-length and live up to your dreams. But I sometimes feel insecure just taking off. For me, our sexual relationship starts when we get out of bed in the morning. The little daily things count.

You will change me. And I will change you. Now I can expend my tender feelings and affection on you infinitely. There is no fear in our intimacy. I look forward to growing in my capacity to give and understand — to spontaneously responding to the flow of emotions between us.

"For this reason a man will leave
his father and mother and be united to his wife,
and they will become one flesh."

Genesis 2:24

What hurts me the most in our relationship is to see you being frustrated.

Today it dawned on me for the first time how important it is to understand your emotions. I have been brought up to be strong. I learned that a boy doesn't cry or show emotions. I felt helpless when I saw you crying or feeling frustrated.

I tried to pinpoint the cause and give a solution to the problem. But afterwards, you felt just as bad. Today I realized that a solution doesn't mean the same to you as it does to me. To you it doesn't matter who has the fault, either. What releases you is to feel the security to express what you feel — and to feel that I understand and accept your feeling.

By sharing thoughts and ideas we widen our relationship. But by sharing emotions, we deepen it.

I must do more than hear what you say; I must listen to what you feel.

Communicate

$\mathcal{W}$omen, I've been told, have a deep need for verbal intimacy. When several evenings pass with projects, T.V., telephone calls, etc. and we haven't had the time to just sit down together and talk casually, I get a desperate feeling inside. When we don't give ourselves the opportunity to converse about new things or talk the old things through, we defeat the purpose of being us. Sometimes, like a child, I need to feel your undivided attention. And I need to share in all the details of your day, and your mind.

I remember the time you first expressed verbally the fact that you had an emotional need to feel loved and accepted by me. You told me specifically what things make you feel emotionally fulfilled. That moment of your supreme openness changed my life. Something turned on in me when I understood that you had just as great emotional needs as I.

But my greatest mistakes have been when I have poorly timed the things I needed to talk to you about. I'm sorry, Honey, I'm learning through trial and error. I believe as I mature in our relationship I'll be able to discern and respond to our ups and downs more creatively, and use my emotions to deepen the quality of my love for you, instead of letting them use me.

"As water reflects
a face, so a man's heart
reflects the man."
Proverbs 27:19

Fidelity

Fidelity is more than just fulfilling my "obligations" as a husband. We easily fall back into the roles where we are no longer sensitive to each other and really aware of the other's presence.

Fidelity is to stay open to change, to be on the move and not fall to the temptation of having the same points of view or saying the same things the rest of my life.

I want to stay alert and alive. When we first fell in love I was willing to change anything about myself.

When I, on our wedding day, promised to love you till death, I thought I could promise to love. But how could I promise something that takes a lifetime to learn?

What I promised was to keep that spark of love aflame by staying alive.

When we were courting, you drove halfway across town to bring me a sketch you'd made and a poem you'd written. It was accompanied by three small garden flowers you'd picked in heaven-only-knows who's garden because you couldn't afford to buy any! You rang the doorbell and handed it to me and disappeared again. Reading it, my heart felt like a marshmallow. And that was typical of the way we related then. We kept each other's hearts soft.

We live together now. We brush our teeth at the same sink. You watch me put on my makeup, and I always end up waiting for you before we can go. When we do something special for each other, it's tempered now by all the small familiar details or irritations of the day or night. We're yoked together in a way that matures us, and in the long run will hopefully mellow our lives. But the periods of boredom or occasions of hurt are rockier than we'd expected.

Moses said God allowed divorce because the people had hard hearts. And that's exactly where my temptation to infidelity begins. Jesus said that in the last days, the love of many would grow cold. Sometimes it scares me how easily my feelings can cool off and influence my commitment. But I'm terrified of ending up with a cold, hard heart.

Surely, in a marriage based on truth, something will come out of our fidelity which has always withstood battles of time and culture, a love greater at its end than its beginning.

25

"Do not
conform
any longer
to
the pattern
of this
world,
but be transformed
by
the renewing
of your mind."

Romans 12:2

Vulnerability

There are three words that are much harder for me to learn than saying, "I love you." They are "I am sorry".

Sometimes I feel the need to share my weaknesses with you like a vulcano inside. I know it is right to do so, but something in me avoids the moment of self-denial and truth about myself. The longer I am quiet, the more I find good reasons to stay the way I am.

Today I shouted, "You married *me* — not a dream guy!" and slammed the door. I felt you expected too much from me. I was tired from a day full of heavy responsibilities.

I am sorry. I've never gotten comfortable myself with the way I am. How could I expect you to?

I need to change and take the risk of saying "Forgive me". Every time *you* do that, you turn on the light in our relationship. I am learning.

And I have found out that you always love me more tenderly when I have dared to say those words.

By nature I am more vulnerable than you. I wear my heart on my sleeve. Even a stranger can read the emotions in my eyes. And I can't hide them from you, even when I want to. For me, one of the joys in marriage is in the protection and comfort you give me from the wounds and hurts of the outside world. But I suppose that same vulnerability that leaves me so exposed is an indirect blessing in our marriage itself. You can read when I'm feeling tense or resentful and you protect me from trying to hide it and repress it. You force me to face it.

I know it's hard for you to accept my intense emotions. And you're aware of my longing to be one with you in yours. I would love to cultivate new areas in life which we could experience with the same feelings. I'm sure a whole new world would take shape between us. But I do also appreciate the growing in self control which is taking place inside me because of you and your cooler attitude to things. We need each other. Let's let that thought renew our commitment and love.

29

"Above all, love
each other deeply,
because love covers
over a multitude
of sins."
1.Peter 4:8

Sometimes I am tempted to think that I know you. Know what you feel, what you think and want to say next. I hear you, but I have stopped listening to you.

I can only love you when I believe in you and stay alive to explore the millions of possibilities still hidden in you. Why do I tend to think in terms of who you were, instead of what you can become?

You want to become something, to materialize your dreams. I want to help you by showing you a direction. Sometimes I think you are unrealistic, and I tell you. But you are destined for something much bigger than you have become until now.

Our future as a couple is dependent on whether the desire to explore surpasses the temptation to resign.

Love is visionary.

*B*en, nobody has ever believed in you more strongly than I do. When we met and fell in love, I had a deep inner assurance of a great potential in you. The person I knew you were on your way to becoming was a very real part of the you that I fell in love with. That has given me some problems in our marriage. I've felt often disappointed or angry. I've sometimes felt discouraged. Once I even felt the hot panic of "it was a mistake." I've hurt you so many times with my selfish ideals. Those hurts have cost us much.

On the other hand, my belief in you has kept me through the hard times and sent me sailing in the eye of the storm. It's given me confidence in "us" and I hope it's given you confidence in yourself. You have already fulfilled so much of what I believed in.

I am fulfilled in your fulfillment. Not because I try to be, or think it would be spiritual to be. But because your successes and growth fulfill me, too. I think that's the way God meant it to be. I feel free and happy being the soil for your growth, and nurturing the seed of things to be in you.

33

"There is
no fear in love.
But perfect love drives
out fear."

1.John 4:18

know that the children's future will depend on the depth of love I give them now. But I am probably more dependent on them than they are on me. There are precious moments in parenthood when I feel contact from heart to heart. I want to hold onto those moments for eternity. But something always comes between and interrupts the sanctity of the moment. When I held the children in my arms today, they got distracted by a puppy.

Most of their day is centered on becoming independent of me. My time with them is centered around binding myself to them by giving myself and making myself vulnerable to them. To be a father is to lay your life into the hands of your child.

I cannot be sure they will become beautiful or intelligent or loveable. I can only love them and hope that love will be awakened in them. That is the risk of being a parent.

Be

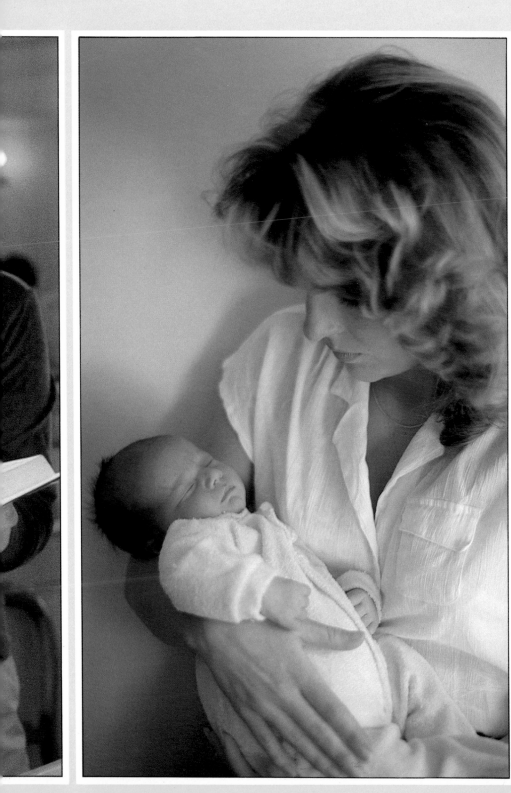

Tiny, precious infant, giving birth to you has been the high point of my life. You are the source of the most intense joy I have ever known, but you have also created the greatest crisis ever. The perpetual exhaustion, feelings of anxiety and inadequacy, feelings of love so great so that I think my heart will burst, but most of all the change in my relationship to your father, has left me confused.

Suddenly, the romance of preparing for your arrival together as a couple has given way to a schism of responsibility. I'm overwhelmed by motherhood. A short while ago I was a wife and expectant mother. Today, I am total mother, immersed in the tyranny of the urgent. Your father tries hard to be understanding and patient, but the frustration is there.

Someday I'll begin to feel normal again, but I suppose the relationship between your father and me will never be the same. You are the paradox of our marriage: You have your way of stealing the time and touch we used to have for each other, and at the same time, you unite us in the most important task and joyous experience of our lives together. You are the beautiful culmination of our love, but you have changed the character and expression of our love forever. It will be even more important that we cultivate our "coupleness" from now on... but just let me catch my breath!

"Sons are
a heritage
from the Lord,
children a reward
from him."

Psalms 127:3

The best gift we can give our children is to show them the joy and pain of being in love with each other, you and me. By spending time with you I show them more than by spending time with them.

Last month, when we went away for a weekend alone we had so much surplus for each other and the children afterwards. And how fun it was to talk and do those things there is never time to do when they are around. I wrote you a poem as I did when we first fell in love. You giggled a lot. We prayed, walked, laughed and did silly things together.

Our work and career take up so much of our time and energy. But our best investment is what we put into our children. Only by practicing ourselves can we give them the real values, teach them to fear God and help them to set real goals for their own lives.

Someday they will be out there on their own. By exemplifying love, openness and vulnerability we may help them become real persons.

Be

Family Together

One of the deepest longings of my heart for us is to create an environment of warmth in our home. Togetherness is not just something we do, it's an attitude we share. It's making personal sacrifices for the good of the whole, attending to small details to make an average day something special, and refusing to make a big deal out of small issues.

I've learned things from your family. I love the way your mother always sets the table with flowers and candles when the children come home, and takes the extra time to decorate the dessert. I want to incorporate your childhood holiday traditions into our family life, and make them meaningful to our girls.

I feel like I've always lacked the quality of imagination, and I've envied those people who had it. But our children love surprises; we all do, I guess. Let's work together on cultivating a sense of expectancy in each other as a man and woman, and in our children.

When I was a child, my mom would sometimes bring a fresh-squeezed glass of orange juice, or banana milk shake before I got out of bed in the morning, or after a long nap. Days can be just as full of fun and loveliness as well as work and accomplishments if somebody makes it a priority. Let's create security by making the most mundane minutes count.

"I urge you to live a life worthy
of the calling you have received.
Be completely humble and gentle;
be patient, bearing with one another in love.
Make every effort to keep the unity of the Spirit
through the bond of peace."

Ephesians 4:1-3

When we first married I thought I could make you change those things I disliked about you. The first crisis came after three years, when I realized you were not going to change.

You still forget the light in the bathroom and squeeze the toothpaste tube the wrong way, you still forget to release the handbrake. Those things irritate me, and I walk off when I feel you do not understand that those things are important to me.

But the real crises are from outside. Sickness. Loss. Financial problems. Spiritual dryness. Those things rob us of our patience with each other and make dim our common vision.

However, I know we cannot avoid the crises by pretending or ignoring them. We have to go through them together. Those crises are the catalysts that lead us into deeper commitment and growth. Through them we become mature persons more capable to give than to take.

I wonder what crises I would have encountered had I stayed single. Thanks for marrying me and staying with me in the crises. Somewhere along the way we found a pearl more precious than the desires of our youth.

Grow

The greatest discovery of our marriage to me is that there is nothing sweeter than having gone through some struggles together and having survived a crisis or two. In the beginning I had rather high expectations. And thinking they were all important, I've strived to keep them alive. But you know what? Instead of the complete personal fulfillment, which I figured marriage was all about, I've found that we are engaged in a vulnerable, variable, incomplete relationship, through which we derive inspiration and courage to reach out to people around us. People with needs just as intimate as our own.

Through the intertwining of our lives, we've learned that we need a community of people, close friends, and most of all God. Through the longing we have for each other, we know how He longs for our love and fellowship.

We believe that our oneness is a sacrament. It is a mystery greater than any crisis which would threaten to destroy it. And yet it is in the crisis that we reach new levels of unity, which in turn are opportunities for creative involvement in the world around us.

"And the God of
all grace, who called you
to his eternal glory in Christ,
after you have suffered a little while,
will himself restore you and make you
strong, firm and steadfast."

1.Peter 5:10

Real Love

Through the leaps forward and the regressions we have made, I have learned that to keep you I must run the risk of losing you.

Love is having enough light to bear the darkness. When my feelings of love die down, it gives me the freedom to love you for being you. When Jesus was at a wedding feast He showed that the second wine is better than the first. The first resources were exhausted, but the latter ones were given as grace.

I accept the fact that we do not express love in the same way. You speak your language. I speak mine. We are two individuals, not united in the way we express love, but in respect and trust in each other's way of loving.

In this sense I begin to understand the love God has for the whole world. With this love it is possible to love everyone and anyone.

Love is individuality made three - dimensional.

*R*ecently, one of my old school friends whom I hadn't seen in ages, remarked, "Marlee, it's fantastic to be together with you, you've 'mellowed out'." And I figure that's just about the most beautiful compliment anybody has ever given me. Because through our life together, the ups and downs, and detours and round-abouts of it all, I've had some sharp corners and rough edges knocked off. And not only does it feel good, but I know it has produced in my life a kind of reality that wasn't there before. It has produced the buddings of real love.

"Mellow" describes somebody who's learned the hard way that it is more important to be kind than to be right. And it describes somebody who's realized through the trials and errors of living that relationships and caring and compassion are really what life is all about. "Mellow" describes somebody who knows that achievement and personal success are empty values.

I know a woman who has five teenage children, and a hectic life of traveling and moving about due to her husband's career. She's about as mellow as can be. I tried once to describe to her what I meant by "mellowed out," and not really catching it, she said, "You mean, worn out?" We laughed.

Worn out, or worn in like a good pair of leather shoes — however you wish to express it. Reaching the point where one unconsciously responds to another person by serving. Where recognizing the needs of others and reaching out is a reflexive impulse, rather than self-imposed sacrifice.

Real love is something that becomes part of your life when you are the least aware of it.

M

"Love is patient,
love is kind. It does
not envy, it does not boast,
it is not proud. It is not rude, it
is not self-seeking, it is not easily angered,
it keeps no record of wrongs. Love
does not delight in evil but rejoices
with the truth. It always protects,
always trusts, always hopes,
always perseveres."

1.Corinthians 13:4-7

And now these three remain:
faith, hope and love.
But the greatest of these is
love.

1.Cor. 13:13